POPULAR SONGS

HAL LEONARD
STUDENT PIANO LIBRARY

POP HITS FOR TWO

10 FRESH AND FUN PIANO DUETS

ARRANGED BY
KEVIN OLSON

T0001363

ISBN 978-1-70515-233-1

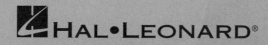

HAL•LEONARD®

Visit Hal Leonard Online at
www.halleonard.com

Contact us:
Hal Leonard
7777 West Bluemound Road
Milwaukee, WI 53213
Email: info@halleonard.com

In Europe, contact:
Hal Leonard Europe Limited
42 Wigmore Street
Marylebone, London, W1U 2RN
Email: info@halleonardeurope.com

In Australia, contact:
Hal Leonard Australia Pty. Ltd.
4 Lentara Court
Cheltenham, Victoria, 3192 Australia
Email: info@halleonard.com.au

FROM THE ARRANGER

One of the most impactful and motivating parts
of my piano training was learning arrangements of
familiar popular songs. Tunes like "Pink Panther"
and "Linus and Lucy" were the ones I would often
choose to play for my friends and family, and the
syncopated rhythms challenged me in ways that
my classical repertoire often didn't. Duet playing
also offers important development in music skills
including solid rhythmic interpretation and balancing
between parts, while offering a social experience
in piano study. Most importantly, integrating both
popular music and duet playing in piano study is
motivating, and keeps the learning process fresh and
fun. I hope that this collection of contemporary pop
duets will be an exciting and enjoyable part of your
piano experience, as it was for me!

Kevin Olson

Kevin Olson
December 2021

CONTENTS

Bad Guy

White shirt now red, my bloody nose
Sleeping, you're on your tippy toes
Creeping around like no one knows
Think you're so criminal...

Words and Music by Billie Eilish O'Connell
and Finneas O'Connell
Arranged by Kevin Olson

Bad Habits

My bad habits lead to wide eyes stare into space
And I know I'll lose control of the things that I say
Yeah, I was lookin' for a way out, now I can't escape
Nothin' happens after two, it's true,
My bad habits lead to you.

Words and Music by Ed Sheeran,
Johnny McDaid and Fred Gibson
Arranged by Kevin Olson

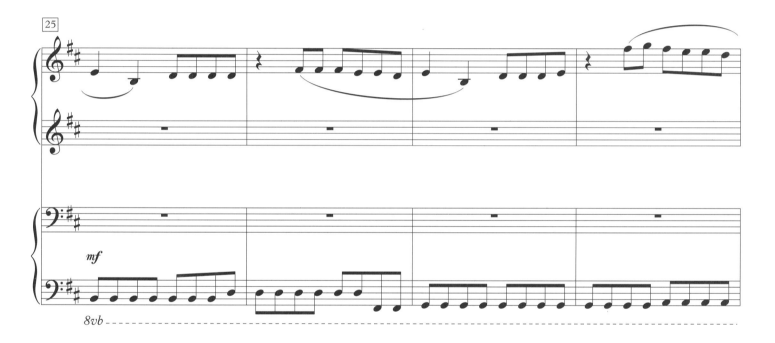

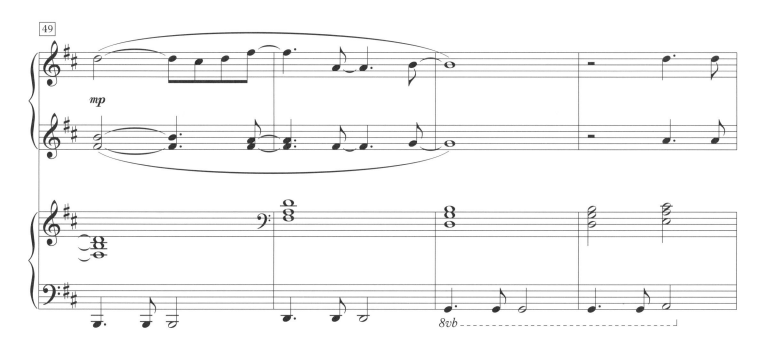

Blinding Lights

I said, ooh, I'm blinded by the lights
No, I can't sleep until I feel your touch
I said, ooh, I'm drowning in the night
Oh, when I'm like this, you're the one I trust.

Words and Music by Abel Tesfaye,
Max Martin, Jason Quenneville,
Oscar Holter and Ahmad Balshe
Arranged by Kevin Olson

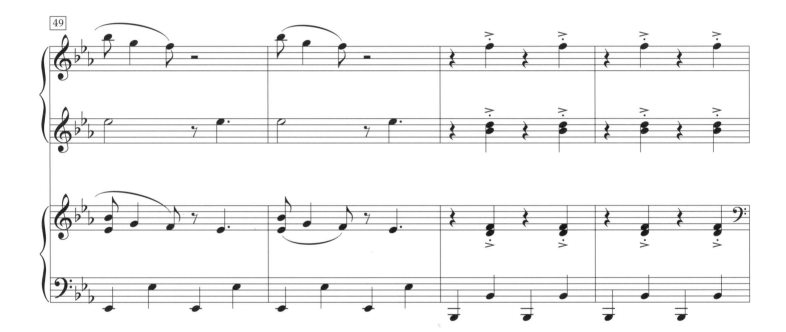

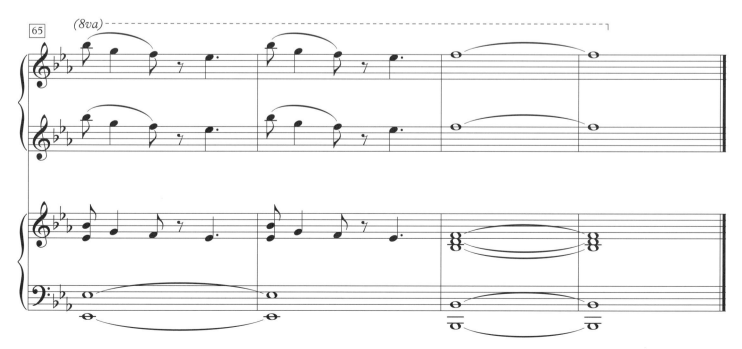

drivers license

...I know we weren't perfect but I've never felt this way for no one
And I just can't imagine how you could be so okay now that I'm gone
Guess you didn't mean what you wrote in that song about me
'Cause you said forever, now I drive alone past your street.

Words and Music by Olivia Rodrigo
and Daniel Nigro
Arranged by Kevin Olson

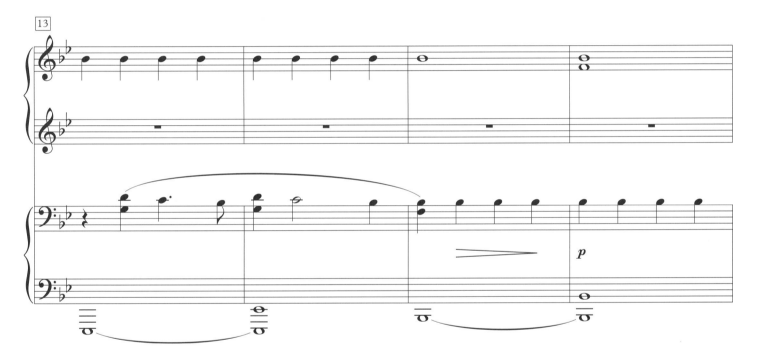

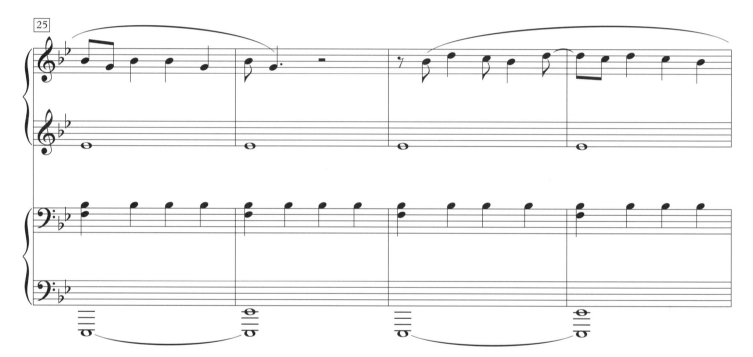

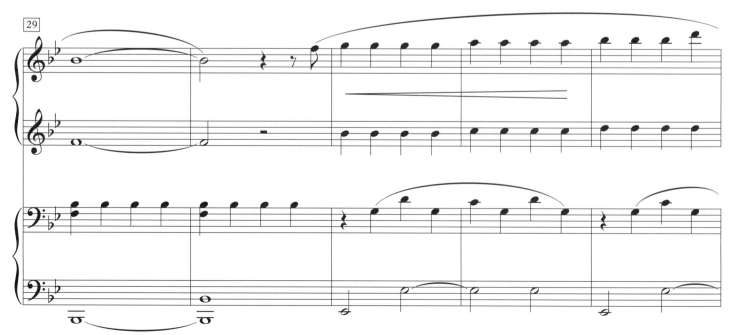

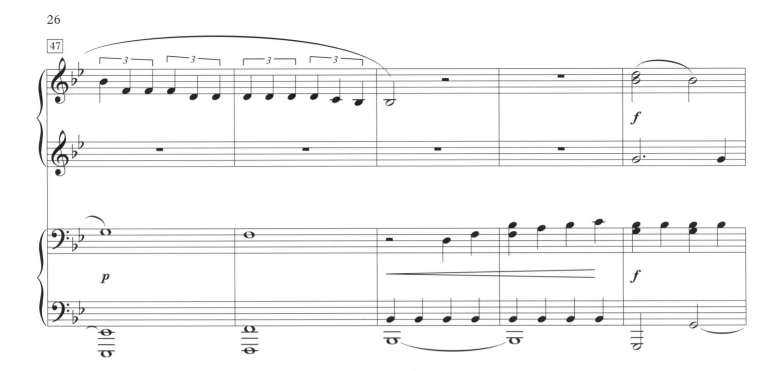

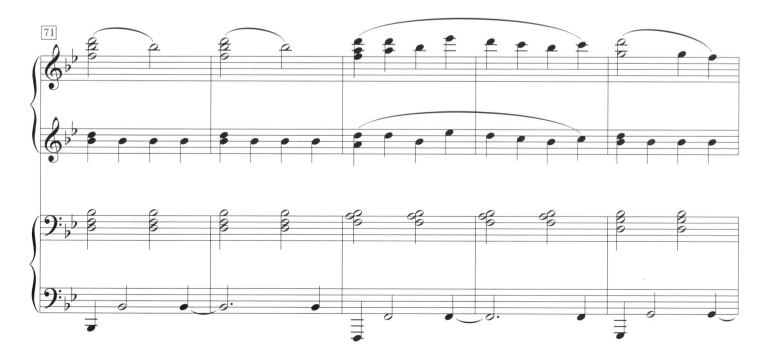

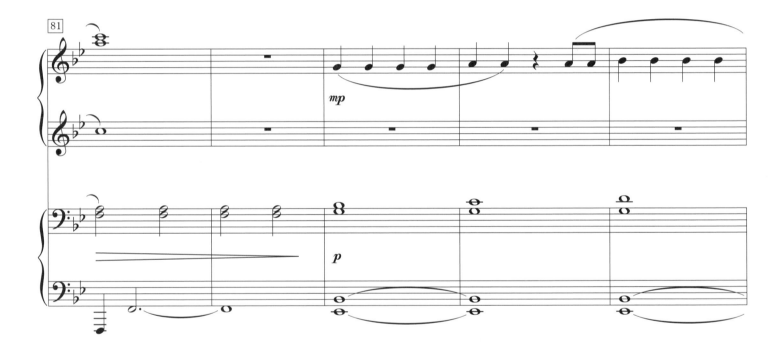

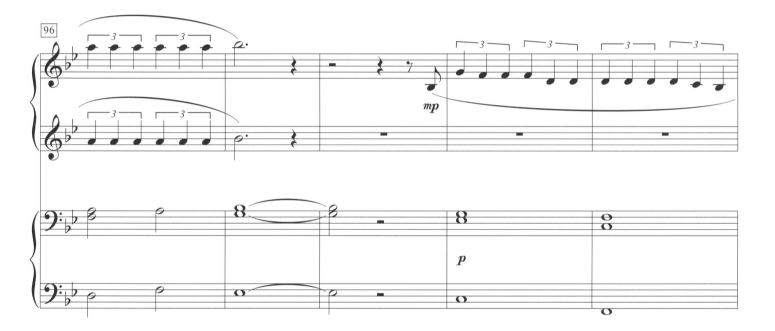

Falling

What am I now? What am I now?
What if I'm someone I don't want around?
I'm falling again, I'm falling again, I'm falling
What if I'm down? What if I'm out?
What if I'm someone you won't talk about?

Words and Music by Harry Styles
and Thomas Hull
Arranged by Kevin Olson

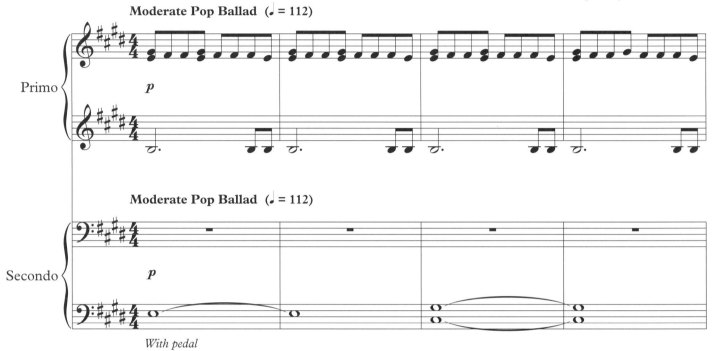

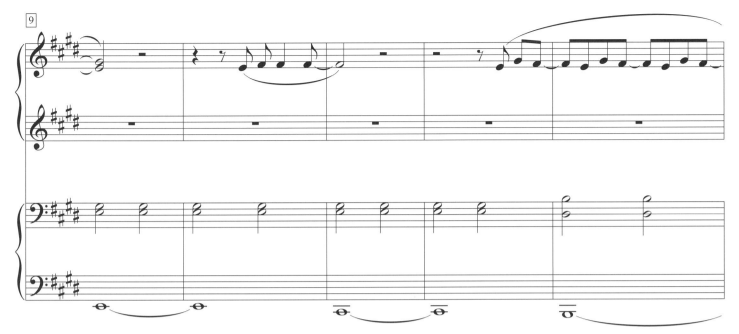

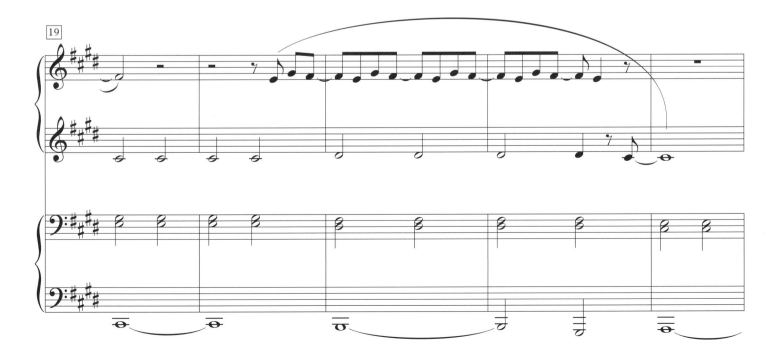

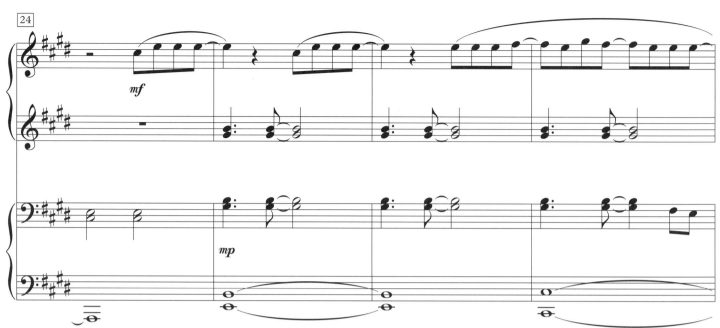

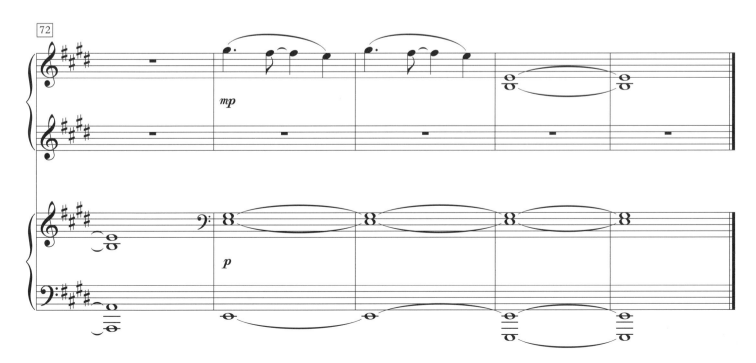

If the World Was Ending

All our fears would be irrelevant
If the world was ending
You'd come over, right?
The sky'd be falling and I'd hold you tight
And there wouldn't be a reason why
We would even have to say goodbye
If the world was ending.

Words and Music by Jonathan Percy Saxe
and Julia Michaels
Arranged by Kevin Olson

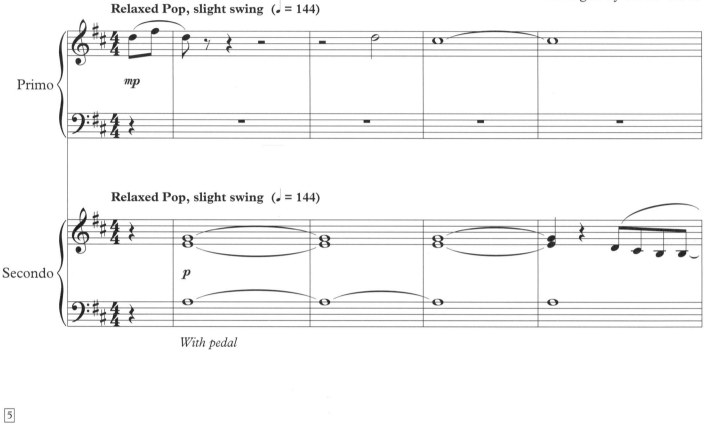

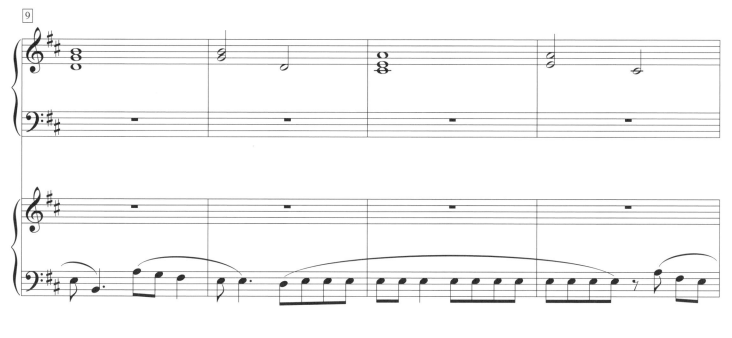

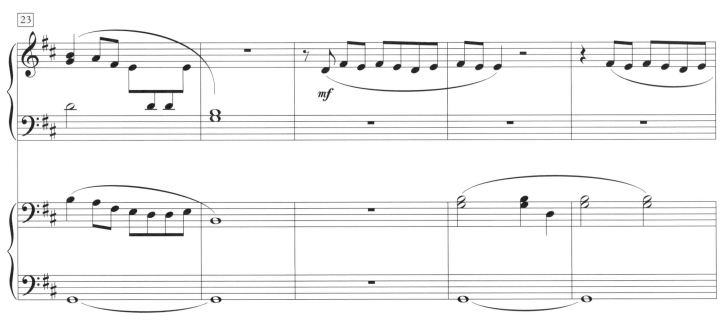

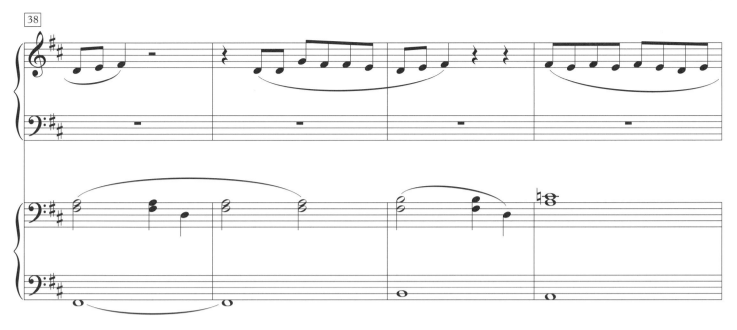

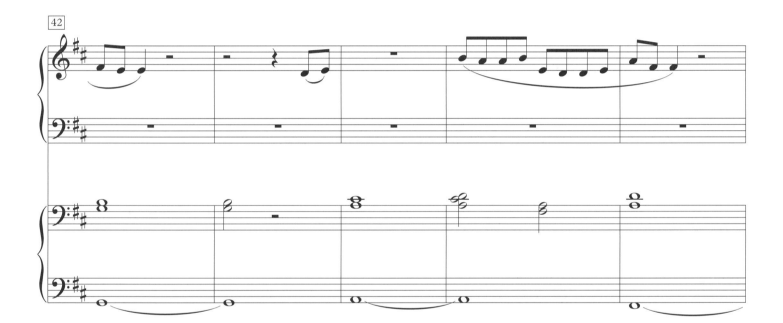

Meant to Be

So, won't you ride with me, ride with me?
See where this thing goes
If it's meant to be, it'll be, it'll be
Baby, if it's meant to be.

Words and Music by Bleta Rexha,
Josh Miller, Tyler Hubbard
and David Garcia
Arranged by Kevin Olson

Memories

Toast to the ones here today
Toast to the ones that we lost on the way
'Cause the drinks bring back all the memories
And the memories bring back, memories bring back you.

Words and Music by Adam Levine,
Jonathan Bellion, Jordan Johnson,
Jacob Hindlin, Stefan Johnson,
Michael Pollack and Vincent Ford
Arranged by Kevin Olson

Mr. Blue Sky

featured in GUARDIANS OF THE GALAXY VOL. 2

Sun is shinin' in the sky
There ain't a cloud in sight
It's stopped rainin' everybody's in the play
And don't you know
It's a beautiful new day, hey hey.

Words and Music by
Jeff Lynne
Arranged by Kevin Olson

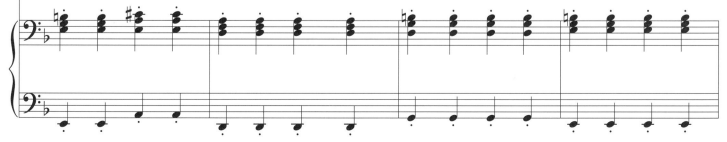

Truth Hurts

Why men great 'til they gotta be great?
Don't text me, tell it straight to my face
Best friend sat me down in the salon chair
Shampoo press, get you out of my hair
Fresh photos with the bomb lighting
New man on the Minnesota Vikings
Truth hurts, needed something more exciting
Bom bom bi bom bi dum dum, ay.

Words and Music by Lizzo,
Eric Frederic, Jesse St. John Geller
and Steven Cheung
Arranged by Kevin Olson

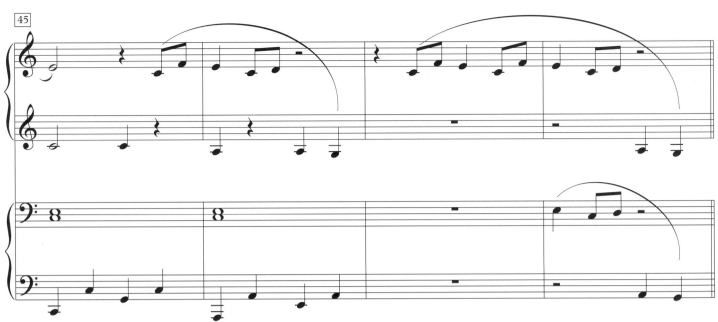